PRESENTED TO

....

FROM

....

DATE

May 25, 1997

....

THE RHYME BIBLE PRAYER BOOK

published by Gold'n'Honey Books
a part of the Questar publishing family

© 1997 by L. J. Sattgast

Illustrations © 1997 by Toni Goffe

International Standard Book Number: 1-57673-054-9

Design by D² DesignWorks
Edited by Melody Carlson and Jennifer Brooks

Printed in the United States of America

For information:
QUESTAR PUBLISHERS, INC.
POST OFFICE BOX 1720
SISTERS, OREGON 97759

97 98 99 00 01 02 03 04 05 — 10 9 8 7 6 5 4 3 2 1

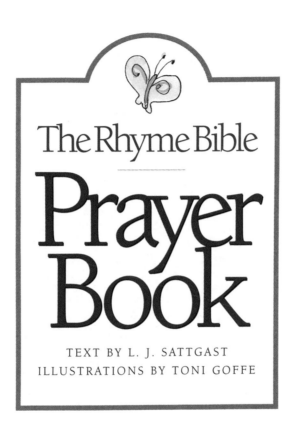

The Rhyme Bible

Prayer Book

TEXT BY L. J. SATTGAST
ILLUSTRATIONS BY TONI GOFFE

Gold 'n' Honey
BOOKS

SISTERS, OREGON

CONTENTS

PSALM 59:16

Morning Praise

It's morning, Lord!
It's morning, Lord!
The sun is shining bright!
It came while I was still asleep
And chased away the night.

I love you, Lord!
I love you, Lord!
I'll sing with all my might,
Because I know that every child
Is precious in your sight!

In the morning
I will sing of your love.

PSALM 59:16

THE 23RD PSALM

He is My Shepherd

Dear God, I'm like your little lamb,
I follow where you lead,
And you are my good shepherd, Lord,
You give me all I need.

You bring me to a grassy field
Where I can run and play.
You lead me to a quiet stream
To take my thirst away.

When, at times, I lose my way
And cannot find the flock,
You guide me with your rod and staff
And show me where to walk.

I might get scared when I must go
Through valleys dark and deep,
Where shadows creep along the path
And frighten little sheep.

But I will listen to your voice,
And this is what I'll hear:
"Don't be afraid, my little lamb,
Remember that I'm near."

Your eyes are always watching
For a hungry wolf or bear,
So I don't need to worry,
Because I know you're there.

Although I'm just a little lamb
I'm sure that I will grow,
And that your love will follow me
Wherever I may go.

But when the sun is sinking low
And day is almost through,
You'll gently take me in your arms,
And this is what you'll do:

You'll look at me with loving eyes
And whisper in my ear,
"Come home with me, my little lamb,
I want you always near!"

The LORD is my shepherd, I shall lack nothing.
He makes me lie down in green pastures,
he leads me beside quiet waters, he restores my soul.
He guides me in paths of righteousness for his name's sake.
Even though I walk through the valley of the shadow of death,
I will fear no evil, for you are with me;
your rod and your staff, they comfort me.
You prepare a table before me in the presence of my enemies.
You anoint my head with oil; my cup overflows.
Surely goodness and love will follow me all the days of my life,
and I will dwell in the house of the LORD forever.

PSALM 23

A Little Prayer

May all the things I think about,
Morning, noon, and night,
And all the words I speak today
Be pleasing in your sight!

———

May the words of my mouth
and the meditation of my heart
be pleasing in your sight,
O LORD, my Rock and my Redeemer.

PSALM 19:14

PSALM 100

A Prayer of Praise

Every creature on the earth,
Shout to God with joy!
Serve him with a happy heart,
Every girl and boy!

God, you made me perfectly,
Just the way I am.
You have called me by my name;
I'm your little lamb!

I will come to worship you
With a thankful heart.
How I love to sing your praise—
Let the music start!

Even though I'm still a child,
You are my best Friend.
When I grow up big and tall
Your faithfulness won't end!

Shout for joy to the LORD, all the earth.
Serve the LORD with gladness; come before him with joyful songs.
Know that the LORD is God.
It is he who made us, and we are his;
we are his people, the sheep of his pasture.
Enter his gates with thanksgiving and his courts with praise;
give thanks to him and praise his name.
For the LORD is good and his love endures forever;
his faithfulness continues through all generations.

PSALM 100

MATTHEW 6:9-13

The Lord's Prayer

Dear Father above,
My heavenly Dad,
Your name is so great,
It makes me feel glad!

I know that your home
Is in heaven above,
Yet here in my heart,
You fill me with love.

You are so mighty,
So big, and so strong!
You love what is right
And hate what is wrong.

Because you are King,
I worship your name.
I pray that all people
Will soon do the same.

Help me to listen
To all that you say,
And teach me, dear Father,
To quickly obey!

Give me the food
I need for today,
And I will say thank you
Each time that I pray.

I'm sorry for doing
Some things that are bad.
I know that it hurts you
And makes you so sad.

You always forgive me
The wrongs that I do.
Please help me, dear God,
To forgive others too.

You made me a promise
That I will not doubt:
When anything tempts me
You'll make a way out.

And so, my dear Father
May these words be true:
All power and glory
Are given to you!

Our Father in heaven,
hallowed be your name,
your kingdom come,
your will be done on earth as it is in heaven.
Give us today our daily bread.
Forgive us our debts,
as we also have forgiven our debtors.
And lead us not into temptation,
but deliver us from the evil one,
for yours is the kingdom, and the power
and the glory forever. Amen.

MATTHEW 6:9-13

PSALM 4:8

Evening Prayer

When shadows drift across the skies
It's time to close my tired eyes.
I do not need to fret or fear,
For you have promised to be near.

Thank you, God, for sleepy night,
And keep me safe till morning's light.
Good night!

I will lie down and sleep in peace,
*for you alone, O L*ORD*,*
make me dwell in safety.

PSALM 4:8